# THE
# CHILDREN'S
# BOOK

## ...for the sake of the children

**A Communication Workbook for Separate Parenting after Divorce**

By Marilyn S. McKnight Erickson
and Stephen K. Erickson

# THE CHILDREN'S BOOK
## ... for the sake of the children

by Marilyn S. McKnight Erickson
and Stephen K. Erickson

Published by
CPI Publishing
West Concord, Minnesota

Cover design:  Greg Wimmer; Ads and Art, Rochester, MN

ISBN 1-881111-02-4

*Printed in the United States of America.*

1 2 3 4 5 6 7 8 9

# TABLE OF CONTENTS

**A note about the authors:**

Marilyn McKnight Erickson is the Director of Family Mediation Services, Inc. in Minneapolis, Minnesota where she has practiced as a family and divorce mediator since 1977. She is a co-author of *FAMILY MEDIATION CASEBOOK*, published by Brunner Mazel, 1988. Ms. McKnight served as President of the Academy of Family Mediators from 1991 to 1992.

Her interest in mediation grew from her experience as a social worker in the suburbs of Minneapolis in the early and mid 1970's. With a case load of mostly divorced families, she observed children struggling in school and experiencing other difficulties during their parents' divorce. Through the eyes of the children, she saw an adversarial divorce system that left families devastated and created "single parents". Much of Ms. Erickson's subsequent work in divorce mediation has focused on helping husbands and wives learn that there need not be victims in divorce; that parents are parents forever; and that parents can function quite well as parents without being married to each other, provided they learn the necessary skills to make separate parenting work. To make separate parenting function more smoothly, Ms. Erickson began in 1984 to suggest that parents exchange a notebook each time the children go from one home to the other. As a 1987 Bush Fellow completing a Master's program in psychology, she further refined the concept by asking parents to answer a questionnaire evaluating *THE CHILDREN'S BOOK*. Both fathers and mothers cited the book as an important tool which allowed them to keep separate lives after divorce, yet provided a method for conducting the "partnership business" of raising children separately. Most of all, it helped the children, because their parents were communicating better and with less conflict. Hopefully, then, in its present form the book will provide a way for the children to emerge as winners. After all, children deserve the best from their parents, even when they are no longer married to each other. *THE CHILDREN'S BOOK* was, indeed, written ". . . for the sake of the children".

Stephen K. Erickson is a mediator and a "recovering attorney". In 1976, after several years as an attorney representing clients in divorce cases, he heard Jim Coogler, an Atlanta lawyer, speak about mediating divorce instead of litigating them. Since that time, he has dedicated his professional career to helping people resolve conflict through mediation. He began practicing Divorce Mediation part time in 1977 and in 1982 he left the traditional practice of law forever.

In 1989, the Idaho Supreme court quoted Mr. Erickson: "Fighting for custody is absurd. The real question is not who is a better or worse parent, but rather, 'What future parenting agreements can both of you agree to so that each of you can be the good loving parents you wish to be.'" Steve Erickson has trained attorneys and therapists to be mediators by showing them a new way of looking at divorce and custody problems. This new approach takes the battle out of divorce and focuses on solutions rather than blame and fault. He is the co-author with Marilyn McKnight of *FAMILY MEDIATION CASEBOOK*, and has published over 25 articles on mediation. He is a founding board member of the Academy of Family Mediators and is its second president.

He believes children should be loved, not the spoils of warfare in the courts.

# FOREWORD

In over 29 years of practicing family law, nothing was more painful than observing the difficulty parents experienced raising their children after separation of divorce. Most parents love their children and most children love both their parents. Most children need both parents to help them achieve their unique potential. This book would benefit all parents but it is especially useful for parents separating after divorce.

This book helps parents work out communicating with each other and with their children in a meaningful way under these difficult circumstances. It is especially useful for young children who perhaps do not fully realize what has happened to their parents.

This book says to each parent, "Let us swallow our pride and our sense of failure and forge ahead and both provide meaningful parenting for the sake of our children".

This book in a very practical way will help both parents eliminate, or at least decrease the enormous pressures that divorce places upon their children.

Chief Justice A.M. "Sandy" Keith
Minnesota State Supreme Court

# INTRODUCTION

*THE CHILDREN'S BOOK* is designed to help you be better parents as you live separately after divorce. Separate parenting means that each parent will have the children at different times, and that there will be periods of time the children are absent from one parent's home. This can make parenting more intense and more complex. (It's hard enough to raise children in just one house.) Two homes require parents to communicate about the children's needs on a regular basis, and have information readily available when parenting them. *THE CHILDREN'S BOOK* is a practical way to accomplish the normal tasks of being a parent. It provides a place to record information about the children for easy reference by both parents as well as a place for parents to communicate with each other about significant events that took place during their time with the children. *THE CHILDREN'S BOOK* travels with the children each time they move from one home to the other so that the parent with the children will have the book for reference.

*THE CHILDREN'S BOOK* is truly a book about your children. It contains information that is unique to them as well as a narrative of your parenting efforts. It will become a keepsake for them as a testimony to your commitment to them. Some day they may understand your commitment and appreciate the effort put forth by both of you during a time of stress and pain for them, and for you as parents.

There is certainly a need to have one place for important information, schedules, teacher's conference dates, medical information, important phone numbers needed by the children, and a host of other things that are necessary to carry on the task of separate parenting. For that parent who spends less time with the children, we have been told *THE CHILDREN'S BOOK* helps to avoid losing contact with important things that happen to the children when they are not with them. Likewise, the parent who spends more time with the children tells us that reading a note from the other parent about what happened during the children's stay helps them talk with the children more easily.

Separate parenting is not easy. In fact, it probably takes more energy than when parenting together. However, it sometimes happens that children have a closer relationship with each parent separately, than might have occurred during the marriage. Separate parenting requires parents to not only learn how to respect the other's personal boundaries, but to also learn to honestly communicate about the children. This respect and honest communication helps the children realize they have a special place in their parents' lives. Thus, *THE CHILDREN'S BOOK* can help demonstrate that parents have not stopped loving their children just because they have stopped loving each other.

Like so many ideas we have used as divorce mediators, the idea for this book came from two parents who used our divorce mediation services in 1978. Not only did they find it difficult to talk to each other, they actually had stopped all forms of contact or conversation and simply exchanged their children without speaking a word. Unfortunately, they found the children burdened with taking on the role of Western Union messengers. Not wanting to put their children in the middle of their own controversy, they started exchanging written notes to each other. Soon, they found that a simple spiral bound notebook, exchanged each time with the children, was a useful way of passing on necessary parenting information to the other parent. From this idea, *THE CHILDREN'S BOOK* grew to its present form.

As you use *THE CHILDREN'S BOOK*, hopefully you will become willing to share information about difficulties you are experiencing with the children, or ideas to try when the children are giving one or both of you trouble, as well as share with each other the joys of parenting. Remember, while you might dislike the other parent, or hate what that person may have done to you in the past, and it is possible to end the marriage partnership, it is never possible to end the parenting partnership. We encourage you to give it your best ". . . for the sake of the children".

# THE CONCEPT OF SEPARATE PARENTING

When parents divorce, the marriage relationship ends and they each begin to plan their future lives as single adults. Yet, because they have children, it is necessary for them to create a new type of relationship as divorced parents who remain partners in the business of raising children. This is all that remains between them and this relationship will keep them connected for the rest of their lives. When parents cooperatively settle their divorce, they have the opportunity to create the terms of this new parenting relationship. Their only contact will be for the sake of their children, and they will find that it is possible to separate the past marriage from the new separate (not single) parenting effort.

Separate parenting, as opposed to single parenting, requires an enormous commitment to cooperate on the part of both parents. They must cooperate to parent their children as best they can, while letting go of all of the other aspects of the former marriage relationship, particularly the negative feelings and deep hurt stemming from the marriage breakup. These negative feelings can often lead to destructive blame and fault finding which creates a stormy parenting partnership. Often, the hurt and anger of the marriage break up contaminates the new parenting effort. In order for children to survive the divorce and emerge as healthy as possible, parents must forgive and stop the blaming and fault finding. They must commit themselves to a new and positive, business-like relationship " . . . for the sake of the children".

Children need the very best each parent has to give particularly during and after a divorce. While divorce is a major factor leading to distress and emotional problems in children, the children's negative reactions are directly related to the level of conflict between their parents. The higher the conflict, the greater their distress. The greatest harm in divorce is for a child to completely lose a relationship with one or the other parent. Children desperately need a relationship with each parent, and each parent must strive to have a respectful and positive separate parenting relationship with the other parent. This is what separate parenting is all about—and it is " . . . for the sake of the children".

3

# ... FOR THE SAKE OF THE CHILDREN

The purpose of this book is twofold. First, it is an informational resource for recording the details about the children's life that parents need to keep organized, especially when living separately. Second, it provides a non-threatening way for parents to communicate with each other as they supply information, in writing, about their children's stay.

The narrative section of this book is designed to help parents communicate information to each other which will be helpful as they parent the children in their separate lives, separate homes, and separate ways.

Some of the information will be about but not limited to these topics:

- Special events
- Achievements
- Difficulties
- School
- Medical Needs
- Reports
- Appointments
- Unusual behavior
- Developmental changes
- Setbacks
- Joys
- Feelings
- Physical and Emotional Needs
- Frustrations
- Opportunities
- Any other information that is considered important to the separate parenting of children.

There may be other concerns to be raised about the children, such as:

- Thoughts about why things are happening with the children.
- Ideas about what to try.
- Narratives about what has been tried.
- Background or hunches about a concern.
- Clarification about what the children said about the other parent.
- Learning different perceptions about an issue.
- Your own questions and answers.

# THE EFFECTS OF DIVORCE ON CHILDREN

All children are affected in some way by divorce. They all experience some trauma from the divorce of their parents. While this cannot be avoided, it can be diminished with the assistance of parents and counselors. Parents first need to understand that children will react negatively to their divorce, and that is normal. Some of these expected reactions are as follows:

**Pre-school children** frequently regress in their development by returning to an earlier stage, usually a recent one. For instance, a recently toilet trained child may begin wetting again, or a child who has become quite social may become "clingy". Children may become more aggressive, or withdraw. It is important for parents to recognize that these changes may occur and it is appropriate to consult with a mental health specialist to learn how to assist the child through these difficult times. Anticipating these expected reactions will hopefully avoid the tendency to blame the other parent for these behavior changes.

**Elementary school children** fear the loss of a parent, and have loyalty conflicts between parents. They may act out in school, and suffer setbacks in school performance. They may even become depressed. Sometimes children think they are at fault for causing the divorce and feel responsible. They may try to get the parents to reconcile and often fantasize about them getting back together.

**Junior high children** can become angry at their parents. They are the ones who are struggling with their identity, and in a sense are being upstaged by their parents' divorce which diverts needed attention from them. They may act out in school and grades may decline. They may also side with one parent (often with the same gender parent) against the other parent. Children from this age group need parental attention and leadership. Unfortunately, their emotionally spent divorcing parents are usually hard pressed to attend to these needs.

**High school children** are already gradually leaving the family, however, the divorce often accelerates this for them. They may spend less and less time at home. They may also become depressed and withdraw to their rooms to cry. Depression is not unusual for this age group. They are often angry with both parents because they see their lives severely disrupted by the divorce.

Few children want their parents to divorce. In fact, most wish, well into their adulthood, that their parents would get back together. Divorce is hard on children of all ages, and parents need to understand this so they may begin to meet the changed needs of their children after divorce.

# DEDICATED TO OUR CHILDREN

Name_____

Birthdate_____ Birth place_____

Weight_____ Length _____ at Birth.

Social Security Number ___/__/___

Name_____

Birthdate_____ Birth place_____

Weight_____ Length _____ at Birth

Social Security Number ___/__/___

Name_____

Birthdate_____ Birth place_____

Weight_____ Length _____ at Birth.

Social Security Number ___/__/___

Name_____

Birthdate_____ Birth place_____

Weight_____ Length _____ at Birth.

Social Security Number ___/__/___

# OUR COMMITMENT

We are dedicating this book to our children as a commitment by each of us to be the best parents we can be after our divorce. This book is part of our best effort to separately parent and give our children a good, healthy upbringing from our two separate homes and lives.

This book is a symbol of our commitment to parenting our children after we are no longer married to each other. We recognize that we are their parents forever, and we agree that we will do our best to carry out the responsibilities, challenges, and privileges of parenting them.

Mom_____ Birthday_____

Dad_____ Birthday_____

# OUR AGREEMENTS ABOUT SEPARATE PARENTING

As parents, we each agree that:

— Our children will have a meaningful relationship with each of us.

— We will communicate with each other directly, either verbally or in writing, and refrain from sending any messages to each other through the children.

— When the children complain to one of us about the other, we will ask the child to discuss it with the other parent, and if the child is uncomfortable we will help the child communicate with the other parent. We will each try to understand the complaint without making a judgment or interfering.

— We understand that our parenting styles are different, that the differences will enhance our children's growth, and we agree to accept and respect each other's differences.

— We will be supportive of each other's parenting and positively encourage the children in their relationship with each of us.

— When parenting problems arise, we will deal with them as parents, just between us.

— We will refrain from discussing our personal lives, and parenting problems and/or differences with the children.

— When we have parenting problems between us that we are unable to resolve, we will seek the services of a family mediator or a neutral expert in family and/or child therapy to assist us in settling the matter.

— If we decide to change any of our parenting agreements, or make new agreements, we will do so in writing and each will retain a copy in order to avoid any misunderstanding about our future agreements. We will sign and date the new agreements and each keep a copy.

— We will respect each other's boundaries. Our separate homes and private lives are no longer joined and we will not enter each other's space without being invited.

— If either of us enter into a new relationship which may affect the children, we will inform the other parent. We will both make an honest effort to assist the children in understanding and adjusting to the new relationship.

# OUR FAMILY

Even though we have decided to divorce, our children will retain the same relatives who care for them and want access to them. We will encourage our children to know their relatives and spend time with them as they grow up. We will each be responsible for our children's access to the relatives on our side of the family. We will also encourage a healthy relationship with their other parent's relatives.

Grandparents are very special to children, and we agree that we will accommodate the needs of the children to continue their relationships with their grandparents. If there are any conflicts about the children's access to their grandparents we agree that we will try to resolve the conflicts between us, and if we are unable we will seek the services of a mediator or a counselor to assist us.

Grandparents on Mom's side of the family:

    Grandfather_____

    Grandmother_____

Grandparents on Dad's side of the family:

    Grandfather_____

    Grandmother_____

Special arrangements for grandparents:

_____

_____

_____

_____

_____

_____

_____

_____

_____

_____

_____

_____

# WHEN ONE OF US REMARRIES

Introducing a significant other person to the children creates another traumatic event for them. First of all, it is a threat to their fantasy that their parents will get back together some day. It also stirs concerns about replacing the other parent and may lead the children to protect the other parent. Nevertheless, parents do remarry and children do adjust. However, the adjustments can become easier if the parents listen to the children's concerns and assure them that even when stepparents enter the family, their parents remain their real parents. Here are some things we can do to assist our children when one of us remarries:

— Assure the other parent that you will not be replacing him or her as a parent.

— Assure the other parent that you want the parenting relationship to continue.

— A remarriage may necessitate the reopening of some issues related to the parenting arrangement.

— Encourage the new spouse to be open to a relationship with the other parent and step back and allow it to happen, at its own pace and in its own time.

— Inform the other parent about your plans and discuss when the children will be told about them.

— Support the entry of this person into the other's life and assist the children with their concerns about it.

— Communicate about the children's needs, questions, and adjustment.

— Clarify with the other parent any information the children may be communicating that you do not understand.

— Be as accepting as possible and avoid getting your own personal feelings mixed with your messages to the children.

— Discuss how the children may react to displays of intimacy in front of them as this may be uncomfortable for them at first.

Other ideas: _____

_____

_____

_____

_____

_____

_____

_____

_____

_____

_____

# PARENTING SCHEDULE

The following schedules are to assure our children that they will have a home with each of us. When they are with one of us, that parent is "on duty" and in charge of all of the routine matters of parenting. When there are unusual or emergency situations, the on duty parent will notify the other of the matter, and we will jointly negotiate any decisions or agreements that need to be made regarding the situation. The schedule is the routine week to week rotating schedule for the children. It will change with holidays and other special days and events agreed upon in advance by each of us. We may each write this schedule on our calendars on the family bulletin board or refrigerator so the children may check it anytime they need.

*Schedules give children a sense of security about a continuing relationship with both parents. Keeping a separate calendar for children posted in a special place in each home at children's eye level is a concrete way to assure the children that both parents are involved with them.*

*Schedules are often based upon the parent's work schedules, children's school and activities, and what will work best for everyone. Sometimes parents want to live in the same school district as the children so they both can be involved in the children's everyday lives. They then build schedules that will work for them and the children. Some sample schedules are given below.*

*Some parents want the children to be in the same home during school and then exchange the children every other weekend from Friday after school until Sunday afternoon or Monday morning, such as:*

*(M=Mom, D=Dad)*

| Month | | | | | | 19__ |
|-------|-------|-------|--------|------|------|------|
| Mon. | Tues. | Wed. | Thurs. | Fri. | Sat. | Sun. |
| M | M | M/D | M | M/D | D | D/M |
| M | M | M/D | M | M | M | M |

16

**OR**

| Month | | | | | | 19__ |
|-------|------|------|-------|------|-----|-----|
| Mon | Tues | Wed | Thurs | Fri | Sat | Sun |
| M | M | M/D | M | M/D | D | D |
| D/M | M | M/D | M | M | M | M |

*Other parents want to each have significant parenting time with the children and choose a schedule that is more equal in the split of time between the homes, such as:*

| Month | | | | | | 19__ |
|-------|------|------|-------|------|-----|-----|
| Mon | Tues | Wed | Thurs | Fri | Sat | Sun |
| M | M | M/D | D | D | D | D |
| D/M | M | M/D | D | D/M | M | M |

**OR**

| Month | | | | | | 19__ |
|-------|------|------|-------|------|-----|-----|
| Mon | Tues | Wed | Thurs | Fri | Sat | Sun |
| M | M | M | M | M/D | D | D |
| D | D | D | D | D/M | M | M |

# SCHEDULING CONSIDERATIONS

There are certainly numerous variations on parenting calendars. When considering calendars for ourselves, we will consider the following factors:

— Our level of cooperation with each other is important to the success of any parenting arrangement. We recognize that the more cooperative we are with each other, the more possible it is to have an equally shared parenting arrangement.

— A more equal arrangement may require us to live in the same school district as each will need to get the children to school on some school mornings.

— Our work schedules are important to the success of the parenting schedule. We will try to work within the constraints of both our schedules.

— Any parenting schedule will work, even if we must travel occasionally in connection with our jobs. Therefore, we both agree to be flexible concerning changes in the schedule due to job related travel.

— Flexibility is important for a workable schedule, and we both agree not to use it as a way to manipulate the schedule.

— The schedule we use now may not be appropriate as the children get older and/or circumstances change. We will be open to the necessity for change, and remember that we may agree to change the schedules if we both choose to do so.

**NOTE:**

*Sometimes scheduling is made easier by agreeing to a regular phone conference between parents to discuss the children's activities for the following week, or to talk about any other parenting issue. Many parents refer to this as "the Sunday Night Phone Call"; a sacred time set aside each Sunday evening to discuss the children. It can be up to an hour in length. Some good rules to use for this phone call are: 1), it must be about children's issues only; and 2), if either is uncomfortable with the conversation, it may be concluded with a statement that it is uncomfortable without further discussion, and a polite goodbye. (It is important to respect the other's judgement about being uncomfortable, and leave it at that.)*

Other ideas:

# OUR PARENTING SCHEDULES

We have agreed upon the following schedules for the dates listed.

*(Fill them in according to your present agreement. Be sure to also list the exchange times so there is a clear understanding about when the children will be picked up or dropped off. Confusion about exchange times can cause unnecessary stress and trauma for the children. Also, remember that delays can not be avoided at times, however, if possible, always telephone the other parent about any delay over 15 minutes.)*

Fill in M=Mom,  D=Dad

| DATES FROM | | | TO | | | |
|---|---|---|---|---|---|---|
| Mon. | Tues. | Wed. | Thur. | Fri. | Sat. | Sun. |
| | | | | | | |
| | | | | | | |
| | | | | | | |
| | | | | | | |
| | | | | | | |

| DATES FROM | | | TO | | | |
|---|---|---|---|---|---|---|
| Mon. | Tues. | Wed. | Thur. | Fri. | Sat. | Sun. |
| | | | | | | |
| | | | | | | |
| | | | | | | |
| | | | | | | |
| | | | | | | |

| Month | | | | | | 19___ |
|-------|-------|-------|-------|------|------|------|
| Mon. | Tues. | Wed. | Thur. | Fri. | Sat. | Sun. |
| | | | | | | |
| | | | | | | |
| | | | | | | |
| | | | | | | |
| | | | | | | |

| Month | | | | | | 19___ |
|-------|-------|-------|-------|------|------|------|
| Mon. | Tues. | Wed. | Thur. | Fri. | Sat. | Sun. |
| | | | | | | |
| | | | | | | |
| | | | | | | |
| | | | | | | |
| | | | | | | |

| Month | | | | | | 19___ |
|-------|-------|-------|-------|------|------|------|
| Mon. | Tues. | Wed. | Thur. | Fri. | Sat. | Sun. |
| | | | | | | |
| | | | | | | |
| | | | | | | |
| | | | | | | |
| | | | | | | |

# ANNUAL SCHEDULE

The regular schedule above sets forth the on duty parent for a typical four week period. We agree, however, that there may be times when we may need to temporarily change the schedule. We agree that if the schedule needs changing, we will be flexible in responding to the other parents needs, but we will not use flexibility as a means to defeat the intent and purpose of the schedules.

Sometimes there are different rotating schedules needed during certain months of the year to accommodate special times. We agree on the following special annual schedule and have signed and dated each agreed upon change.

Fill in: M=Mom, D=Dad

| Month | | | | | | 19__ |
|-------|------|------|------|------|------|------|
| Mon. | Tues. | Wed. | Thur. | Fri. | Sat. | Sun. |
| | | | | | | |
| | | | | | | |
| | | | | | | |
| | | | | | | |

| Month | | | | | | 19__ |
|-------|------|------|------|------|------|------|
| Mon. | Tues. | Wed. | Thur. | Fri. | Sat. | Sun. |
| | | | | | | |
| | | | | | | |
| | | | | | | |
| | | | | | | |

| Month | | | | | | 19___ |
|-------|-------|-------|-------|------|------|------|
| Mon. | Tues. | Wed. | Thur. | Fri. | Sat. | Sun. |
| | | | | | | |
| | | | | | | |
| | | | | | | |
| | | | | | | |
| | | | | | | |

| Month | | | | | | 19___ |
|-------|-------|-------|-------|------|------|------|
| Mon. | Tues. | Wed. | Thur. | Fri. | Sat. | Sun. |
| | | | | | | |
| | | | | | | |
| | | | | | | |
| | | | | | | |
| | | | | | | |

| Month | | | | | | 19___ |
|-------|-------|-------|-------|------|------|------|
| Mon. | Tues. | Wed. | Thur. | Fri. | Sat. | Sun. |
| | | | | | | |
| | | | | | | |
| | | | | | | |
| | | | | | | |
| | | | | | | |

| Month | | | | | | 19__ |
|-------|-------|-------|-------|-------|-------|-------|
| Mon. | Tues. | Wed. | Thur. | Fri. | Sat. | Sun. |
| | | | | | | |
| | | | | | | |
| | | | | | | |
| | | | | | | |
| | | | | | | |

| Month | | | | | | 19__ |
|-------|-------|-------|-------|-------|-------|-------|
| Mon. | Tues. | Wed. | Thur. | Fri. | Sat. | Sun. |
| | | | | | | |
| | | | | | | |
| | | | | | | |
| | | | | | | |
| | | | | | | |

| Month | | | | | | 19__ |
|-------|-------|-------|-------|-------|-------|-------|
| Mon. | Tues. | Wed. | Thur. | Fri. | Sat. | Sun. |
| | | | | | | |
| | | | | | | |
| | | | | | | |
| | | | | | | |
| | | | | | | |

| Month | | | | | | 19___ |
|-------|-------|------|-------|------|------|-------|
| Mon. | Tues. | Wed. | Thur. | Fri. | Sat. | Sun. |
| | | | | | | |
| | | | | | | |
| | | | | | | |
| | | | | | | |
| | | | | | | |

| Month | | | | | | 19___ |
|-------|-------|------|-------|------|------|-------|
| Mon. | Tues. | Wed. | Thur. | Fri. | Sat. | Sun. |
| | | | | | | |
| | | | | | | |
| | | | | | | |
| | | | | | | |
| | | | | | | |

| Month | | | | | | 19___ |
|-------|-------|------|-------|------|------|-------|
| Mon. | Tues. | Wed. | Thur. | Fri. | Sat. | Sun. |
| | | | | | | |
| | | | | | | |
| | | | | | | |
| | | | | | | |
| | | | | | | |

# HOLIDAY SCHEDULES

The following holiday schedules will be posted in each of our homes for the children to refer to at any time.

Indicate "M" (Mom) or "D" (Dad) for holidays celebrated.

| Significant Holiday | Even Year | Odd Year |
|---|---|---|
| New Year's Day | | |
| Spring Break | | |
| Easter | | |
| Passover | | |
| Memorial Day Weekend | | |
| Fourth of July | | |
| Labor Day Weekend | | |
| Rosh Hashana | | |
| Halloween | | |
| Thanksgiving | | |
| Hanukkah | | |
| Christmas Eve | | |
| Christmas Day | | |
| Winter Break | | |
| Mother's/Father's Day | | |
| Children's Birthdays | | |
| | | |
| | | |
| | | |
| | | |
| | | |
| | | |

# SCHOOL YEAR AND DAYS OFF

School Year Begins_____Ends_____

School days off:

Columbus Day Observed:_____

Teacher's Convention:_____

Veteran's Day Observed:_____

Martin Luther King's Birthday Observed:_____

President's Day:_____

_____

_____

_____

_____

_____

Winter Break:_____

_____

Spring Break:_____

_____

# SCHOOL YEAR AND DAYS OFF

School Year Begins_____Ends_____

School days off:

Columbus Day Observed:_____

Teacher's Convention:_____

Veteran's Day Observed:_____

Martin Luther King's Birthday Observed:_____

President's Day:_____

_____

_____

_____

_____

_____

Winter Break:_____

_____

Spring Break:_____

_____

# SCHOOL YEAR AND DAYS OFF

School Year Begins_____Ends_____

School days off:

Columbus Day Observed:_____

Teacher's Convention:_____

Veteran's Day Observed:_____

Martin Luther King's Birthday Observed:_____

President's Day:_____

_____

_____

_____

_____

_____

Winter Break:_____

_____

Spring Break:_____

_____

# SCHOOL YEAR AND DAYS OFF

School Year Begins_____Ends_____

School days off:

Columbus Day Observed:_____

Teacher's Convention:_____

Veteran's Day Observed:_____

Martin Luther King's Birthday Observed:_____

President's Day:_____

_____

_____

_____

_____

_____

Winter Break:_____

_____

Spring Break:_____

_____

# VACATIONS WITH MOM AND WITH DAD

Vacations With Mom:

Dates:_____

_____

_____

Plans:_____

_____

_____

_____

Vacations With Dad

Dates:_____

_____

_____

Plans:_____

_____

_____

_____

# VACATIONS WITH MOM AND WITH DAD

Vacations With Mom:

Dates:_____

_____

_____

Plans:_____

_____

_____

_____

Vacations With Dad

Dates:_____

_____

_____

Plans:_____

_____

_____

_____

# VACATIONS WITH MOM AND WITH DAD

Vacations With Mom:

Dates:_____

_____

_____

Plans:_____

_____

_____

_____

Vacations With Dad

Dates:_____

_____

_____

Plans:_____

_____

_____

_____

# VACATIONS WITH MOM AND WITH DAD

Vacations With Mom:

Dates:_____

_____

_____

Plans:_____

_____

_____

_____

Vacations With Dad

Dates:_____

_____

_____

Plans:_____

_____

_____

_____

## SUMMER VACATIONS AND CHILDREN'S ACTIVITIES

We agree that we will begin to plan for the children's summer break early enough for us to decide on camps and our summer vacations. We agree that we will communicate with each other early in the year to discuss ideas and plans for the children during the summer.

_____

_____

_____

_____

_____

_____

_____

_____

_____

_____

_____

_____

_____

# SUMMER VACATIONS AND CHILDREN'S ACTIVITIES

_____

_____

_____

_____

_____

_____

_____

_____

_____

_____

_____

_____

_____

_____

# HEALTH INFORMATION

Names of all of the doctors, dentists, and specialists of each of our children.

| Professional: | Child: | Specialty: | Phone: |
|---|---|---|---|
| | | | |
| | | | |
| | | | |
| | | | |
| | | | |
| | | | |
| | | | |
| | | | |
| | | | |

Health Insurance Company_____I.D.#_____

Specific Medical Information (Chronic problems, Allergies, etc.)

_____

_____

_____

_____

_____

# HEALTH INFORMATION

Names of all of the doctors, dentists, and specialists of each of our children.

| Professional: | Child: | Specialty: | Phone: |
|---|---|---|---|
| | | | |
| | | | |
| | | | |
| | | | |
| | | | |
| | | | |
| | | | |
| | | | |
| | | | |
| | | | |

Health Insurance Company_____I.D.#_____

Specific Medical Information (Chronic problems, Allergies, etc.)

_____

_____

_____

_____

_____

# MEDICATIONS AND PRESCRIPTIONS

| Date | Name of Medicine | For Whom | For What Symptoms |
|------|------------------|----------|-------------------|
|  |  |  |  |
|  |  |  |  |
|  |  |  |  |
|  |  |  |  |
|  |  |  |  |
|  |  |  |  |
|  |  |  |  |
|  |  |  |  |
|  |  |  |  |
|  |  |  |  |
|  |  |  |  |
|  |  |  |  |
|  |  |  |  |
|  |  |  |  |
|  |  |  |  |
|  |  |  |  |
|  |  |  |  |
|  |  |  |  |
|  |  |  |  |
|  |  |  |  |
|  |  |  |  |
|  |  |  |  |
|  |  |  |  |
|  |  |  |  |
|  |  |  |  |
|  |  |  |  |
|  |  |  |  |

# MEDICATIONS AND PRESCRIPTIONS

| Date | Name of Medicine | For Whom | For What Symptoms |
|------|------------------|----------|-------------------|
|      |                  |          |                   |
|      |                  |          |                   |
|      |                  |          |                   |
|      |                  |          |                   |
|      |                  |          |                   |
|      |                  |          |                   |
|      |                  |          |                   |
|      |                  |          |                   |
|      |                  |          |                   |
|      |                  |          |                   |
|      |                  |          |                   |
|      |                  |          |                   |
|      |                  |          |                   |
|      |                  |          |                   |
|      |                  |          |                   |
|      |                  |          |                   |
|      |                  |          |                   |
|      |                  |          |                   |
|      |                  |          |                   |
|      |                  |          |                   |
|      |                  |          |                   |
|      |                  |          |                   |
|      |                  |          |                   |
|      |                  |          |                   |
|      |                  |          |                   |

# MEDICATIONS AND PRESCRIPTIONS

| Date | Name of Medicine | For Whom | For What Symptoms |
|------|------------------|----------|-------------------|
|      |                  |          |                   |
|      |                  |          |                   |
|      |                  |          |                   |
|      |                  |          |                   |
|      |                  |          |                   |
|      |                  |          |                   |
|      |                  |          |                   |
|      |                  |          |                   |
|      |                  |          |                   |
|      |                  |          |                   |
|      |                  |          |                   |
|      |                  |          |                   |
|      |                  |          |                   |
|      |                  |          |                   |
|      |                  |          |                   |
|      |                  |          |                   |
|      |                  |          |                   |
|      |                  |          |                   |
|      |                  |          |                   |
|      |                  |          |                   |
|      |                  |          |                   |
|      |                  |          |                   |
|      |                  |          |                   |
|      |                  |          |                   |
|      |                  |          |                   |

# MEDICATIONS AND PRESCRIPTIONS

| Date | Name of Medicine | For Whom | For What Symptoms |
|------|------------------|----------|-------------------|
|      |                  |          |                   |
|      |                  |          |                   |
|      |                  |          |                   |
|      |                  |          |                   |
|      |                  |          |                   |
|      |                  |          |                   |
|      |                  |          |                   |
|      |                  |          |                   |
|      |                  |          |                   |
|      |                  |          |                   |
|      |                  |          |                   |
|      |                  |          |                   |
|      |                  |          |                   |
|      |                  |          |                   |
|      |                  |          |                   |
|      |                  |          |                   |
|      |                  |          |                   |
|      |                  |          |                   |
|      |                  |          |                   |
|      |                  |          |                   |
|      |                  |          |                   |
|      |                  |          |                   |
|      |                  |          |                   |
|      |                  |          |                   |
|      |                  |          |                   |

# MEDICAL RECORDS

The following information is requested to be filled in by parents on every camp, sports, and other registration sheet which requires a statement of the child's health. Recording it here keeps each of us from the hassle of resurrecting it from the medical files each time it is requested.

Child's Name_____

Health History: (Give approximate dates)

| | |
|---|---|
| Ear Infections _____ | Chicken Pox _____ |
| Heart Disease/Defects _____ | Measles _____ |
| Convulsions _____ | German Measles _____ |
| Diabetes _____ | Mumps _____ |
| Bleeding/Clotting _____ | Hay Fever _____ |
| Hypertension _____ | Ivy Poisoning _____ |
| Psychiatric Treatment _____ | Insect Stings _____ |
| Mononucleosis _____ | Penicillin _____ |
| Asthma _____ | Other _____ |

Immunization History: (Give month and year)

|  | Basic | Boosters |
|---|---|---|
| Pertussis (Whooping cough) | _____ | _____ |
| Tetanus/Diptheria combined:DPT | _____ | _____ |
| OR | | |
| Tetanus/Diptheria combined:DT | _____ | _____ |
| OR | | |
| Tetanus | _____ | _____ |
| Oral Polio (Salk) | _____ | _____ |
| Measles (hard, red, Rubella) | _____ | _____ |
| Mumps | _____ | _____ |
| Other | _____ | _____ |

Date of Most Recent Tuberculin Test_____

# MEDICAL RECORDS

Child's Name_____

Health History:  (Give approximate dates)

Ear Infections _____      Chicken Pox _____
Heart Disease/Defects _____      Measles _____
Convulsions _____      German Measles _____
Diabetes _____      Mumps _____
Bleeding/Clotting _____      Hay Fever _____
Hypertension _____      Ivy Poisoning _____
Psychiatric Treatment _____      Insect Stings _____
Mononucleosis _____      Penicillin _____
Asthma _____      Other _____

Immunization History:  (Give month and year)

|  | Basic | Boosters |
| --- | --- | --- |
| Pertussis (Whooping cough) | _____ | _____ |
| Tetanus/Diptheria combined:DPT | _____ | _____ |
| OR |  |  |
| Tetanus/Diptheria combined:DT | _____ | _____ |
| OR |  |  |
| Tetanus | _____ | _____ |
| Oral Polio (Salk) | _____ | _____ |
| Measles (hard, red, Rubella) | _____ | _____ |
| Mumps | _____ | _____ |
| Other | _____ | _____ |

Date of Most Recent Tuberculin Test_____

# MEDICAL RECORDS

Child's Name_____

Health History:  (Give approximate dates)

Ear Infections _____     Chicken Pox _____
Heart Disease/Defects _____     Measles _____
Convulsions _____     German Measles _____
Diabetes _____     Mumps _____
Bleeding/Clotting _____     Hay Fever _____
Hypertension _____     Ivy Poisoning _____
Psychiatric Treatment _____     Insect Stings _____
Mononucleosis _____     Penicillin _____
Asthma _____     Other _____

Immunization History:  (Give month and year)

| | Basic | Boosters |
|---|---|---|
| Pertussis (Whooping cough) | _____ | _____ |
| Tetanus/Diptheria combined:DPT | _____ | _____ |
| OR | | |
| Tetanus/Diptheria combined :DT | _____ | _____ |
| OR | | |
| Tetanus | _____ | _____ |
| Oral Polio (Salk) | _____ | _____ |
| Measles (hard, red, Rubella) | _____ | _____ |
| Mumps | _____ | _____ |
| Other | _____ | _____ |

Date of Most Recent Tuberculin Test_____

# MEDICAL RECORDS

Child's Name_____

Health History:  (Give approximate dates)

Ear Infections _____     Chicken Pox _____
Heart Disease/Defects _____     Measles _____
Convulsions _____     German Measles _____
Diabetes _____     Mumps _____
Bleeding/Clotting _____     Hay Fever _____
Hypertension _____     Ivy Poisoning _____
Psychiatric Treatment _____     Insect Stings _____
Mononucleosis _____     Penicillin _____
Asthma _____     Other _____

Immunization History:  (Give month and year)

|  | Basic | Boosters |
| --- | --- | --- |
| Pertussis (Whooping cough) | _____ | _____ |
| Tetanus/Diptheria combined:DPT | _____ | _____ |
|     OR |  |  |
| Tetanus/Diptheria combined:DT | _____ | _____ |
|     OR |  |  |
| Tetanus | _____ | _____ |
| Oral Polio (Salk) | _____ | _____ |
| Measles (hard, red, Rubella) | _____ | _____ |
| Mumps | _____ | _____ |
| Other | _____ | _____ |

Date of Most Recent Tuberculin Test_____

# MEDICAL RECORDS

Child's Name_____

Health History:  (Give approximate dates)

Ear Infections _____     Chicken Pox _____
Heart Disease/Defects _____     Measles _____
Convulsions _____     German Measles _____
Diabetes _____     Mumps _____
Bleeding/Clotting _____     Hay Fever _____
Hypertension _____     Ivy Poisoning _____
Psychiatric Treatment _____     Insect Stings _____
Mononucleosis _____     Penicillin _____
Asthma _____     Other _____

Immunization History:  (Give month and year)

|  | Basic | Boosters |
|---|---|---|
| Pertussis | _____ | _____ |
| Tetanus/Diptheria combined:DPT | _____ | _____ |
| OR | | |
| Tetanus/Diptheria combined:DT | _____ | _____ |
| OR | | |
| Tetanus | _____ | _____ |
| Oral Polio (Salk) | _____ | _____ |
| Measles (hard, red, Rubella) | _____ | _____ |
| Mumps | _____ | _____ |
| Other | _____ | _____ |

Date of Most Recent Tuberculin Test_____

# FINANCIAL INFORMATION

## Children's Social Security Numbers

| Child: | Social Security Number |
|--------|------------------------|
|        |                        |
|        |                        |
|        |                        |
|        |                        |

## Children's Savings Accounts

| For Whom: | Institution: | Account# | Responsible Parent: |
|-----------|-------------|----------|---------------------|
|           |             |          |                     |
|           |             |          |                     |
|           |             |          |                     |
|           |             |          |                     |
|           |             |          |                     |

## Children's Accounts for Higher Education

| For Whom: | Institution: | Account# | Responsible Parent: |
|-----------|-------------|----------|---------------------|
|           |             |          |                     |
|           |             |          |                     |
|           |             |          |                     |
|           |             |          |                     |

# SPECIAL FINANCIAL ARRANGEMENTS FOR CHILDREN:

Money held in trust under Uniform Gift to Minors Act

| For Whom: | Institution: | Account# | Responsible Parent: |
|-----------|--------------|----------|---------------------|
|           |              |          |                     |
|           |              |          |                     |
|           |              |          |                     |
|           |              |          |                     |
|           |              |          |                     |
|           |              |          |                     |

Savings Bonds

| For Whom: | Institution: | Account# | Responsible Parent: |
|-----------|--------------|----------|---------------------|
|           |              |          |                     |
|           |              |          |                     |
|           |              |          |                     |
|           |              |          |                     |
|           |              |          |                     |
|           |              |          |                     |

Other financial information and agreements about our children's savings and higher education funds:_____

_____

_____

_____

_____

# OUR CHILDREN'S IMPORTANT FRIENDS AND RELATIVES

| Child | Friend/Relative | Phone Number |
|---|---|---|
| | | |
| | | |
| | | |
| | | |
| | | |
| | | |
| | | |
| | | |
| | | |
| | | |
| | | |
| | | |
| | | |
| | | |
| | | |
| | | |
| | | |
| | | |
| | | |
| | | |
| | | |
| | | |
| | | |
| | | |
| | | |
| | | |

# OUR CHILDREN'S IMPORTANT FRIENDS AND RELATIVES

| Child | Friend/Relative | Phone Number |
|-------|-----------------|--------------|
|  |  |  |
|  |  |  |
|  |  |  |
|  |  |  |
|  |  |  |
|  |  |  |
|  |  |  |
|  |  |  |
|  |  |  |
|  |  |  |
|  |  |  |
|  |  |  |
|  |  |  |
|  |  |  |
|  |  |  |
|  |  |  |
|  |  |  |
|  |  |  |
|  |  |  |
|  |  |  |
|  |  |  |
|  |  |  |
|  |  |  |
|  |  |  |
|  |  |  |
|  |  |  |

# OUR CHILDREN'S IMPORTANT FRIENDS AND RELATIVES

| Child | Friend/Relative | Phone Number |
|-------|-----------------|--------------|
|       |                 |              |
|       |                 |              |
|       |                 |              |
|       |                 |              |
|       |                 |              |
|       |                 |              |
|       |                 |              |
|       |                 |              |
|       |                 |              |
|       |                 |              |
|       |                 |              |
|       |                 |              |
|       |                 |              |
|       |                 |              |
|       |                 |              |
|       |                 |              |
|       |                 |              |
|       |                 |              |
|       |                 |              |
|       |                 |              |
|       |                 |              |
|       |                 |              |
|       |                 |              |
|       |                 |              |
|       |                 |              |
|       |                 |              |
|       |                 |              |

# CHILD CARE INFORMATION

Day Care or Child Care Arrangements

Child_____

Name of Provider_____

Address and Phone_____

Schedule_____Fees_____

Comments_____

_____

_____

_____


Child_____

Name of Provider_____

Address and Phone_____

Schedule_____Fees_____

Comments_____

_____

_____

_____

# CHILD CARE INFORMATION

Day Care or Child Care Arrangements

Child_____

Name of Provider_____

Address and Phone_____

Schedule_____Fees_____

Comments_____

_____

_____

_____

Child_____

Name of Provider_____

Address and Phone_____

Schedule_____Fees_____

Comments_____

_____

_____

_____

# CHILD CARE INFORMATION

Day Care or Child Care Arrangements

Child_____

Name of Provider_____

Address and Phone_____

Schedule_____Fees_____

Comments_____

_____

_____

_____

Child_____

Name of Provider_____

Address and Phone_____

Schedule_____Fees_____

Comments_____

_____

_____

_____

# CHILD CARE INFORMATION

Day Care or Child Care Arrangements

Child_____

Name of Provider_____

Address and Phone_____

Schedule_____Fees_____

Comments_____

_____

_____

_____

Child_____

Name of Provider_____

Address and Phone_____

Schedule_____Fees_____

Comments_____

_____

_____

_____

# THOSE WHOM WE TRUST WITH OUR CHILDREN

<u>Babysitters</u>

Name_____Phone_____

Name_____Phone_____

Name_____Phone_____

Name_____Phone_____

<u>Each parent's emergency contacts</u>

For Mom:

Name_____Phone_____

Name_____Phone_____

Name_____Phone_____

For Dad:

Name_____Phone_____

Name_____Phone_____

Name_____Phone_____

# THOSE WHOM WE TRUST WITH OUR CHILDREN

<u>Babysitters</u>

Name_____Phone_____

Name_____Phone_____

Name_____Phone_____

Name_____Phone_____

<u>Each parent's emergency contacts</u>

For Mom:

Name_____Phone_____

Name_____Phone_____

Name_____Phone_____

For Dad:

Name_____Phone_____

Name_____Phone_____

Name_____Phone_____

# THOSE WHOM WE TRUST WITH OUR CHILDREN

<u>Babysitters</u>

Name_____Phone_____

Name_____Phone_____

Name_____Phone_____

Name_____Phone_____

<u>Each parent's emergency contacts</u>

For Mom:

Name_____Phone_____

Name_____Phone_____

Name_____Phone_____

For Dad:

Name_____Phone_____

Name_____Phone_____

Name_____Phone_____

# THOSE WHOM WE TRUST WITH OUR CHILDREN

## Babysitters

Name_____Phone_____

Name_____Phone_____

Name_____Phone_____

Name_____Phone_____

## Each parent's emergency contacts

### For Mom:

Name_____Phone_____

Name_____Phone_____

Name_____Phone_____

### For Dad:

Name_____Phone_____

Name_____Phone_____

Name_____Phone_____

# THOSE WHOM WE TRUST WITH OUR CHILDREN

<u>Babysitters</u>

Name_____Phone_____

Name_____Phone_____

Name_____Phone_____

Name_____Phone_____

<u>Each parent's emergency contacts</u>

For Mom:

Name_____Phone_____

Name_____Phone_____

Name_____Phone_____

For Dad:

Name_____Phone_____

Name_____Phone_____

Name_____Phone_____

# SCHOOL INFORMATION

We agree that we will communicate with each other when we receive the school calendar, and if necessary meet with each other and work out our calendars for the school year to accommodate any special days off or other issues surrounding the school year.

| Child | Name of School | Phone Number |
|---|---|---|
|  |  |  |
|  |  |  |
|  |  |  |
|  |  |  |
|  |  |  |

| Child | Conference Dates | Teacher |
|---|---|---|
|  |  |  |
|  |  |  |
|  |  |  |
|  |  |  |

| Child |  |  |
|---|---|---|
|  |  |  |
|  |  |  |
|  |  |  |
|  |  |  |
|  |  |  |

# SCHOOL INFORMATION

| Child | Name of School | Phone Number |
|-------|----------------|--------------|
|       |                |              |
|       |                |              |
|       |                |              |
|       |                |              |

| Child | Conference Dates | Teacher |
|-------|------------------|---------|
|       |                  |         |
|       |                  |         |
|       |                  |         |
|       |                  |         |

| Child |  |  |
|-------|--|--|
|       |  |  |
|       |  |  |
|       |  |  |
|       |  |  |

# SCHOOL INFORMATION

| Child | Name of School | Phone Number |
|-------|----------------|--------------|
|       |                |              |
|       |                |              |
|       |                |              |
|       |                |              |

| Child | Conference Dates | Teacher |
|-------|------------------|---------|
|       |                  |         |
|       |                  |         |
|       |                  |         |
|       |                  |         |

| Child |  |  |
|-------|--|--|
|       |  |  |
|       |  |  |
|       |  |  |
|       |  |  |

# EXTRACURRICULAR ACTIVITIES

We agree that we will discuss with each other the registration of the children for their extracurricular activities. When we agree on the activity we will cooperate with each other in transportation, etc. When we do not agree on the activity, the parent supporting the particular activity will have full responsibility for transportation, etc., and the other parent will not interfere.

**Child**_____Subject_____

Coach/Teacher_____

Address_____Phone_____

Day_____Time_____

Comments_____

_____

_____

**Child**_____Subject_____

Coach/Teacher_____

Address_____Phone_____

Day_____Time_____

Comments_____

_____

_____

# EXTRACURRICULAR ACTIVITIES

**Child**_____Subject_____

Coach/Teacher_____

Address_____Phone_____

Day_____Time_____

Comments_____

_____

_____

_____


**Child**_____Subject_____

Coach/Teacher_____

Address_____Phone_____

Day_____Time_____

Comments_____

_____

_____

_____

# EXTRACURRICULAR ACTIVITIES

**Child**_____Subject_____

Coach/Teacher_____

Address_____Phone_____

Day_____Time_____

Comments_____

_____

_____

_____


**Child**_____Subject_____

Coach/Teacher_____

Address_____Phone_____

Day_____Time_____

Comments_____

_____

_____

_____

# EXTRACURRICULAR ACTIVITIES

**Child**_____Subject_____

Coach/Teacher_____

Address_____Phone_____

Day_____Time_____

Comments_____

_____

_____


**Child**_____Subject_____

Coach/Teacher_____

Address_____Phone_____

Day_____Time_____

Comments_____

_____

_____

We will place the schedules for these events in the pocket of this book, or make copies for each of us to have at our separate homes.

# IMPORTANT BIRTHDAYS OF SPECIAL FRIENDS AND RELATIVES

We understand that children often need their parents to remind them of the special days of their friends or relatives that they would be very disappointed to miss or forget.

| Child: | Person: | Birth Date: |
|---|---|---|
| | | |
| | | |
| | | |
| | | |
| | | |
| | | |
| | | |
| | | |
| | | |
| | | |
| | | |
| | | |
| | | |
| | | |
| | | |
| | | |
| | | |
| | | |
| | | |
| | | |
| | | |
| | | |
| | | |

# IMPORTANT BIRTHDAYS OF SPECIAL FRIENDS AND RELATIVES

| Child: | Person: | Birth Date: |
|--------|---------|-------------|
|        |         |             |
|        |         |             |
|        |         |             |
|        |         |             |
|        |         |             |
|        |         |             |
|        |         |             |
|        |         |             |
|        |         |             |
|        |         |             |
|        |         |             |
|        |         |             |
|        |         |             |
|        |         |             |
|        |         |             |
|        |         |             |
|        |         |             |
|        |         |             |
|        |         |             |
|        |         |             |
|        |         |             |
|        |         |             |
|        |         |             |
|        |         |             |
|        |         |             |
|        |         |             |
|        |         |             |
|        |         |             |

# BOOKS TO READ

*Parents often ask for books to read to their children or for their children to read themselves about separation and divorce. The following list is not meant to include all of the available books but some which we have learned about from parents, therapists and others who work with divorcing families. There is space provided at the bottom for additional book suggestions of others.*

THE DINOSAUR'S DIVORCE, by Laureen Krasny Brown and Marc Brown. Children of all ages enjoy this book.

THE BOYS AND GIRLS BOOK OF DIVORCE, by Richard Gardner. A book for older elementary and teens to read.

GROWING UP WITH DIVORCE, by Neil Kalter. Another book that helps children adjust to their parents divorce.

HOW IT FEELS WHEN PARENTS DIVORCE, by Jill Krementz. This book contains stories of children's experiences when their parents divorced.

*Parents also ask for books that they can read to better understand what their children are experiencing and how to parent their children during separation and after divorce. The following are just a few of the books that parents have indicated are helpful to them.*

THE DIVORCE BOOK FOR PARENTS, by Vicki Lansky. Practical tips about parenting after divorce is what this book is about.

MOM'S HOUSE, DAD'S HOUSE, by Isolina Ricci. This book offers a lot of information and answers many of the questions parents have about shared parenting after divorce.

71

SURVIVING THE BREAKUP, by Joan Kelly and Judith Wallerstein. The research findings about children's reactions to divorce reported in this book are widely accepted and corroborated by other research.

_____

_____

_____

_____

_____

_____

_____

_____

_____

_____

_____

_____

_____

# NARRATIVE OF INFORMATION

This section is for us to write messages to each other of important facts, details, or events that occurred while the children were with each of us. By writing a few lines just before the children move to each of our homes, the other parent will have information about the children that the children will not need to be responsible to communicate. It may also answer any questions that arise when the children recount the time with one of us and clarify any misperceptions they may have.

Date:_____

_____

_____

_____

_____

_____

_____

_____

_____

_____

_____

_____

_____

_____

Date:_____

_____

_____

_____

_____

_____

_____

_____

_____

_____

_____

_____

_____

_____

_____

_____

_____

_____

_____

_____

_____

_____

_____

_____

_____

Date:_____

Date:_____

Date:_____

_____

_____

_____

_____

_____

_____

_____

_____

_____

_____

_____

_____

_____

_____

_____

_____

_____

_____

_____

_____

_____

_____

_____

_____

Date:_____

Date:_____

Date:_____

Date:_____

Date:_____

_____

_____

_____

_____

_____

_____

_____

_____

_____

_____

_____

_____

_____

_____

_____

_____

_____

_____

_____

_____

_____

_____

_____

_____

_____

_____

Date:_____

Date:_____

_____

_____

_____

_____

_____

_____

_____

_____

_____

_____

_____

_____

_____

_____

_____

_____

_____

_____

_____

_____

_____

_____

_____

_____

Date:_____

Date:_____

_____

_____

_____

_____

_____

_____

_____

_____

_____

_____

_____

_____

_____

_____

_____

_____

_____

_____

_____

_____

_____

_____

_____

_____

Date:_____

Date:_____

Date:_____

Date:_____

Date:_____

Date:_____

Date:_____

Date:_____

Date:_____

_____

_____

_____

_____

_____

_____

_____

_____

_____

_____

_____

_____

_____

_____

_____

_____

_____

_____

_____

_____

_____

_____

_____

_____

Date:

Date:_____

Date:_____

_____

_____

_____

_____

_____

_____

_____

_____

_____

_____

_____

_____

_____

_____

_____

_____

_____

_____

_____

_____

_____

_____

_____

Date:_____

_____

_____

_____

_____

_____

_____

_____

_____

_____

_____

_____

_____

_____

_____

_____

_____

_____

_____

_____

_____

_____

_____

Date:_____

Date:_____

Date:_____

Date:_____

Date:_____

Date:_____

Date:_____

Date:_____

Date:_____

Date:_____

Date:_____

Date:_____

Date:_____

Date:_____

_____

_____

_____

_____

_____

_____

_____

_____

_____

_____

_____

_____

_____

_____

_____

_____

_____

_____

_____

_____

_____

_____

Date:_____

_____

_____

_____

_____

_____

_____

_____

_____

_____

_____

_____

_____

_____

_____

_____

_____

_____

_____

_____

_____

_____

Date:_____

Date:_____

_____
_____
_____
_____
_____
_____
_____
_____
_____
_____
_____
_____
_____
_____
_____
_____
_____
_____
_____
_____
_____
_____
_____
_____
_____
_____

Date:_____

_____

_____

_____

_____

_____

_____

_____

_____

_____

_____

_____

_____

_____

_____

_____

_____

_____

_____

_____

_____

_____

_____

_____

Date:_____

Date:_____

_____

_____

_____

_____

_____

_____

_____

_____

_____

_____

_____

_____

_____

_____

_____

_____

_____

_____

_____

_____

_____

_____

Date:_____

_____

_____

_____

_____

_____

_____

_____

_____

_____

_____

_____

_____

_____

_____

_____

_____

_____

_____

_____

_____

_____

_____

_____

_____

_____

Date:_____

## INTER-HOUSE COMMUNICATION ENVELOPE

*This envelope is for:  Children's Health Insurance Cards, Membership Cards, Health Records, Copies of Birth Certificates, Social Security Cards, etc.*

*It is also a means of sending school notices and special papers of the children back and forth when the school does not send duplicates to parents separately.*